LIFE

IS

SIMPLE

Written by Mark L. Hatalla

ISBN: 978-0-6151-5266-0

I am a Fire Captain in a major city and have been a Firefighter for almost 30 years. I have responded to thousands of alarms from major fires to minor medical calls and everything in between.

Fire Departments protect lives and property. We respond to almost anything you can imagine. We provide services to everyone regardless of their income, age, nationality, and religion.

We are proud when we save a life, happy when we help someone, and disappointed when there is nothing we can do. All of these things can happen in one shift or within a few hours.

We live away from our families every third day. Most Fire Departments work 24 hours on duty and 48 hours off duty. The 24 hours on duty we live, eat, sleep, respond to emergencies, and do everything together as one unit. Each of our lives depends on the members of our Company. That's our Fire Department family.

Because we are away from our immediate families much of the time, we must balance these two families. In addition to balancing the time we spend with each family we must balance the emotional ups and downs. The incidents we respond to are hard to explain to someone who has never experienced it. Because of this both families are important for support.

As true with everyone, our views are based on our experiences. Firefighters are fortunate or unfortunate to be exposed to a large variety of experiences good and bad to provide assistance.

"Dedication"

This is dedicated to my youngest brother Bart, who passed away August 24, 2005 at 44 years old. Even though we lived about 800 miles apart we often talked about life issues. We discussed everything from religion, health, family, finance, relationships, work, and issues in the world.

We would talk about what each other would do if we were in different situations. We understood each other's views and opinions. We had very similar beliefs. I understand now we were balancing our lives. Happiness is found when your life is balanced and you share it with others.

Bart had his life in balance. He was able to balance his religious beliefs, family, friends, work, entertainment, and finances based on the priorities he set. He was truly happy. I miss our conversations and his thoughts.

"Table of Contents"

"Introduction"

Life is simple. Life it self is simple. As we grow older we complicate our lives by our choices and actions or lack of actions.

We make choices that affect our lives, some have long-term affects and others have short-term affects. Every day we make decisions about religious beliefs, health, relationships, and finance.

We are creatures of habit. Just about everything we do, we do because that's the way we always have done something. Habits are not always bad. We have a lot of good habits, but the bad habits get more attention. Bad habits get more attention because we would like to change them while our good habits are taken for granted.

We can control our habits. You will know if your life is out of balance. You have the ability to balance your life. Sometimes we do not have the determination to commit ourselves to making changes. We must change things that prevent us from being happy.

The key to enjoying your life is keeping your life in balance. The more things in your life that are balanced the happier you will be. When life throws some thing at you, if your life is in balance, a simple adjustment will take care of the issue and you will remain balanced. Remember: "life is simple, we make it complicated".

PART I

The Four Aspects Of Life

"Four Aspects"

There are four aspects in your life that need to be balanced. They need to be balanced with each other as well as within themselves. The four aspects are religious beliefs, health, relationships, and finance.

Everyone has these four aspects in their lives regardless of their age, sex, religion, race, income, environment, political views, or social status. All of these factors may affect the four aspects in your life but it does not change them.

Depending on the direction you take in life with your occupation and values, you set your priorities and one of these four aspects is more dominant then the others. Even though it is more dominant then the others it still must be balanced with the others. If the dominant aspect becomes your only concern the other aspects will suffer. This may affect your ability to fulfill the goals of your dominant aspect.

Religious beliefs are what give you direction. It provides meaning and a direction for you to follow through your life. It also gives your life a beginning, middle, end, and after life.

Health is the vehicle we use to follow our direction. We use our bodies to follow and live our lives according to our direction. We must maintain good health for our bodies. Relationships with family and friends are our support systems. They encourage us when we are down and acknowledge us when we achieve something. They help us to continue following our direction.

Finance is the means. Finance in a business aspect helps us meet our wants and needs. The wants are forever changing. The basic needs remain primarily the same, food, shelter, love, and etc.

These four aspects must be balanced if one demands more than the other, the other three have to compensate.

"Religious Belief"

Regardless of your religious belief, there are similarities among all religions. They all have a beginning to life, life on earth, an end of life, and life after death.

How we were created affects our beliefs on how we are to live our lives and what happens at the end of our lives. There are many different religions with many different religious beliefs. Even with the many religious differences there are still many religious similarities that direct our lives.

In order to have direction in your life we must believe that Jesus Christ is the Son of God. If you do not believe in Jesus Christ and God you cannot believe in the teachings of Jesus Christ.

"For God so loved the world, that he gave his only begotten Son, that whosoever believeth in him should not perish but have everlasting life." John 3:16

We attend church to learn of Jesus Christ teachings. Just learning of his teachings is not enough. We must do our best to follow his teachings. Once you learn the right path, we should follow it, every day. We are not perfect. We all make mistakes or do things we know we should not have done. We are all sinners. "But God commendeth his love toward us, in that, while we were yet sinners, Jesus Christ died for us." Romans 5:8

This does not mean we can go through life doing whatever we want to do without consequences. It means our sins will be forgiven. Jesus Christ died upon a cross for you so that you would not burn in the lake of fire. He died so that you could be saved forever. He paid the penalty for your sins. "For the wages of sin is death; but the gift of God is eternal life through Jesus Christ our Lord." Romans 6:23

We pray for different things. We pray for guidance and strength or support. God has a plan for our life on earth. Sometimes we lose our direction in life and pray for assistance. When we have fulfilled our purpose on earth, God brings us to him. There is a place in heaven for those who believe in him.

We do not know what plan God has for us, or how long we will live on earth. In any case, life is short. We must live our lives to serve God's plan. That is not to say that we cannot live our lives as we want to. It means we live our lives at the grace of God to serve him. Some things in life are not worth fighting about. We hurt each other and mistreat each other every day. This creates conflicts and unhappiness. There must be a balance between our religious beliefs and the way we live our lives.

We attend church services to learn about our religious beliefs and spiritual support. There is a master plan created by our creator. There is a plan for our lives. We cannot change it. We just try to live our lives in accordance to a plan we have never seen. We pray for guidance and receive a sense of direction. We call this our fate.

We should live our lives according to our beliefs all of the time. We are only human, we are not perfect, nor can we be perfect all of the time. Follow your beliefs. Live your beliefs. Going to church every Sunday and doing other activities with the church does not make you a believer or more religious than everyone else. It just gives you perfect attendance. If you do not follow and live your beliefs, you are not a believer. It's not always easy but, you must follow your belief's to be balanced. Remember: "doing right is not always easy, but it is always right".

"Health"

We have a direct affect on our health. Eating habits, exercise, entertainment, sleep habits, and etc. all effect our health. When we are born our bodies are usually healthy. As we grow older we develop habits that affect our health. As our bodies begin to get out of balance it tells us by gaining weight, chest pains, difficulty breathing, and other symptoms that indicate something is not right. We do not always accept the fact that something is wrong. Usually we do not change our habits to balance our health until it is far enough out of balance that it becomes a serious health problem.

This doesn't mean you cannot do certain things. It just means that you have to do them in moderation. When you abuse your body your health will suffer. Our bodies are self-adjusting. Our bodies will try to adjust to our misuse until it can no longer do so, then health problems begin.

We can do little things to maintain our health. Take the stairs every so often instead of the elevator. Take a walk. You don't have to have a personal trainer to add more physical activity to your life. Listen to your body if you have aches and pains after doing something. It means your body is not used to do that activity. Our activity level begins to slow down as we age. So we must make adjustments to maintain our physical condition.

Because our activity levels slow down, so does our ability to burn fat. We must follow the signs our bodies give us. The signs are different for everyone. We are unique; we all eat different foods and have different activity levels. You must listen to your body.

We are in control of our bodies. We control what we put into it. We also control our physical activities to keep it in good physical shape. Work hours, sleeping habits, and stress also affect our health. These are all just part of life; everyone has these types of issues. Some people learn how to handle these issues by balancing them. They cannot be eliminated, they have to be balanced. Remember: "short term actions or lack of action, have long term effects".

"Relationships"

O f the four aspects of life, relationships may be the most difficult to balance because it "takes two". We can only control our actions; we cannot control the actions of someone else.

We can create an environment to encourage a favorable behavior. No matter what we do the behavior of someone else can only be changed by that person. All of us live our lives in different environments throughout our lives. As things change in our lives so does the environments in which we live.

Our parents create our first environment. When we were born that was the only environment we knew. Our parents created an environment where we feel loved, safe, and secure where we can grow and learn.

When we become parents we try to create a similar type environment for our children. We create an environment based on our experiences and influences from our lives.

Our experiences and influences in life come from several sources. It starts with our parents and other family members. As we become more independent we develop more relationships with people outside our immediate family. They include friends, co-workers, people with similar interests, and people we don't know. All of these people have an influence on our lives. We learn from other people and their experiences as well as ours. We don't have to make the same mistakes to learn. Everybody makes mistakes, some people never learn. Life is a continuing learning experience. We learn something new everyday even if we don't realize it. Remember: "you learn the most, after you know it all".

"Family"

Family and close friends are our support mechanism. When we are having a difficult time our family and friends are there to talk to. Relationships are based on trust and commitment. The stronger the commitment the stronger the relationship and vice versa, without trust there really is no relationship.

Relationships are important to enjoying life and having a happy life. They work both ways. If we have accomplished something that we are proud about and share it with someone we feel good. If someone else shares one of their accomplishments with us, we feel good because they shared it with us.

We communicate to each other in different ways besides verbal. The reaction can be observed and sometimes the reaction can make us happier than the verbal acknowledgements. Some of our actions just put a smile on a face and that's all we need to know. When we hug or kiss or make a funny face we usually see a smile. You can tell you made that person happy without saying a word, and in return you feel happy too. Sharing happiness involves sharing with other people.

Relationships can be very complicated because it takes two. That means there are two different opinions as well as two different responses. You can only control your actions and feelings. You cannot make someone else agree with you, like you, love you, or share your feelings. We can create an environment to make people feel comfortable, secure, and welcome but they control their feelings. We can only accept people for who they are. Past experiences form our relationships, good ones as well as bad ones. Everyone must follow their own path. You must understand their past through trust and commitment.

When we start our own families, we reflect on our family environments. We carry-over the good and try to improve on the things we thought were not so good. As times change so does the family environment. This creates one of many differences of opinion. What type of environment do you want to live in and what do you want to pass on to your children?

Everyone gets hurt feelings during their life, that's just part of life. No one wants to be hurt again, so we protect ourselves. Sometimes this protecting will not allow someone into our lives for fear of being hurt again. In a relationship you must understand that the other person has been hurt before and assure them that you will not treat them the same way. It takes time. Remember: "the stronger the commitment, the stronger the relationship, and vice versa".

"Friends"

Friends are very important to enjoying life. Their experiences and influence are just as important as the experiences and influences from your family. Your friends can offer something to your life your family can not. Friends are not as emotionally involved in your life as your family. They can provide the view of a third person in a situation to provide a more objective point of view. We have a lot of friends but close friends are hard to find. A close friend is like a family member.

During our early life our family environment has the greatest influence on our lives. As we become more independent our friends have more of an influence on our lives. As teens our friends are more important. Sometimes the friendships are more important than the environment and influence it has on our lives. Once we learn about responsibility and accountability we begin to choose our friends and environments more wisely. As adults our experiences and influences have a different importance.

When we enter the work environment we learn a lot more about different relationships. We have co-workers and supervisors in a work related environment. We also learn more about authority, respect, and job related performance. These things existed in our family environment but they have different consequences in a work environment. Your family is always your family but jobs and friends may come and go. Good friends are like family, they're always your friend. Remember: "you are given authority, you earn respect"

"Finance"

Money is a necessity of life. Money is our standard for goods and services. We go to work to earn money. We trade our time for a salary. We take our salary and begin to divide it to meet our living expenses.

Living expenses consist of the necessities such as food, shelter, utilities, and etc. These are the things you have to have to survive. We also enjoy other practical things such as vacations, vehicles, computers, and etc. Then we have things of lesser value that we spend our money on such as alcohol, tobacco, drugs, and etc. These are all individual choices; it's your time, your money, and your life.

If your finances get out of balance it usually affects everything else, thus making you're life very complicated. Planning is the key to financial stability. Not just the short-term but long-term as well.

Short-term planning is for those things that occur while you are still working. House repairs, vehicle maintenance, savings account, and living expenses are examples of short-term financial issues.

Long term planning is investing for your future. When you retire your expenses should be less, but so is your income. A little money invested every month is a better investment than the same amount invested once a year. When you invest, your money makes money.

There are also some things that are both short term and long-term expenses. Short-term planning is monthly expense to pay off long-term investments. When you purchase a house, get married, have children, college, and etc. These things affect your short-term budget, with a long-term expense.

Balancing a budget is easier said than done. Actually the solution is easy, the process is difficult. There are only three possible solutions, increase income, reduce expenses, or a combination of both. The processes are difficult, work more hours or decide what you must give up. But always remember to pay yourself first. Always set money aside for expected/unexpected expenses.

Some people believe the more money you have the happier you are. There are a lot of things that have more value than what money can buy. You can have all the money in the world; if you have no one to share it with no one cares. The happiness that money brings only lasts as long as the money. Remember: "we work to live, we don't live to work".

PART II

Life

Life goes on, we cannot stop it and we cannot speed it up. We just do our best to live it. We can only control how we live it by the things we do or don't do and how we act.

Life has its ups and downs that is just what life is about. How we respond to the ups and downs affects our happiness and how we live our lives. Any change produces stress; it doesn't matter if it is a good change or a bad change. Change of any kind still affects the stress in our lives.

Our direction in life is predetermined by God; we are just part of his master plan. We attend church services to learn of his teachings and pray for his assistance and direction. God controls our fate.

When it's your time to leave this earth, it's your time. I have seen many vehicle accidents where the vehicles are totally destroyed and no one was injured. Other accidents the vehicles where barely scratched and someone died.

Things happen for a reason. We may not understand why things happen. It's our fate. We do our best to live our lives but fate always changes our plans.

How we make adjustments to our life can make life simple or make it more complicated. There are no "do overs", once it has happened, its history. We must learn from our mistakes or the mistakes of others. It is foolish to keep making the same mistake over and over again.

We cannot take back the hurt we caused someone; we can only avoid hurting someone in the future. We cannot get back the time we should have spent or the things we should have done with someone before they died. Once they're gone it's too late.

Life is short. We must enjoy every day as much as we can. One day will be our last day on earth. It may be today. What in life is important to you? Are you happy with your life? What can you change to balance your life?

We can adjust our actions and balance our lives if we have the correct attitude, perspective, and priorities. These vary for everyone and are always changing. As we grow older our priorities and perspectives change. Remember: "learn from the past, live for the future".

"Attitude"

Having the right "attitude" can keep things simple or make things more complicated. We are affected by other people's attitudes, just as our attitudes affect other people.

If we project a happy, friendly, and positive attitude when we communicate with others, most of the time the same attitude will be returned to us. If we project a spiteful, bitter, and negative attitude chances are that type of attitude will be returned.

We cannot directly control other people's attitudes. But if we project a positive attitude even when we must deal with a negative attitude, we will remain balanced. It is difficult to get upset with someone who is being nice to you.

This is very easy to prove. Through the course of the day greet people you don't know or have never seen before. It doesn't have to be a lengthy conversation. Just say, "Hello, how are you doing?" See the reaction you get. It might just be a smile, but chances are it will be a positive reaction. And you will also feel good as well.

Our attitudes are formulated by the environment we live in as well as the people we associate with. We watch other people; we watch their reactions to different situations. Sometimes we say, "if that was me I would have ……" other times we think "I wish I could have reacted that way". You are the only one who can change your attitude. Remember: "be a good example, you never know who is watching".

"Perspective"

How we look at things gives us all a different perspective of our lives. We tend to look at what things we don't have, instead of what things we have.

We tend to look at people who have more things than we have and wish we had more of what they have. But when you reverse the perspective things look very different.

Take a look at what things you have. And what things other people don't have. Instead of worrying about what things you don't have. You become very thankful for the things you have.

Your perspective is not limited to money and possessions. Your health, family, friends, beliefs, values, and accomplishments, all affect your perspective. You also affect the perspectives that others have by following your example and your outlook on life.

Every now and then you need to take time for yourself and reflect on your life. Look at your religious beliefs and ask: "am I moving in the right direction?" And what can I do to improve my perspective? Think about your health "is my body trying to tell me something that I ignored?" The last two aspects of life require a little more thought because they involve other people and a majority of our daily life. We have to understand their perspective before we can share ours. Sometimes they're very different.

Family and friends are important to our daily lives and we are important to them as well. There are many questions that you can ask yourself. When you think about your actions or lack of actions you will find that you could have done things differently. But don't just think of things you could have done better, remember the things that made someone happy and the things that you enjoyed doing.

There are reasons why we budget our money the way we do. Everyone does it differently for different reasons. Our priorities may be similar but the reasoning will vary. Everyone has financial obligations and different ways of meeting those obligations. You must balance your obligations to live within your means or life becomes very stressful and affects all of the aspects of your life.

Sometimes it may be necessary to look at a situation from the view of a third party. Look at the facts of a situation not the emotions. Make decisions based on the facts and support the emotional feelings.

As you reflect back on your life and think about things you should have done or could have done. Also remember the things you have done, were they the right things to do? Could they have been done better? Remember: "you can not lie to yourself".

"Priorities"

We take a simple life and complicate it. We do this with "priorities". We want to do everything and have everything. Of course this is not possible. So we set priorities. This is where the real balancing act comes into play. To balance our priorities we must also balance our time and money.

There is only so much time in a day. We try to manage our time to accommodate our desires. This is different for everyone. Depending on how well your life is balanced affects how well you can manage your desires.

Some people say you have to sacrifice something so you can do something else. I don't agree with the terminology sacrifice. I believe you set priorities and make adjustments to balance your priorities.

To adjust your priorities you must set goals. Some long term and some short term. We use our priorities to achieve our goals. As we achieve our short term goals we must set new ones. It is a continuing process but as our short term goals are met we feel good about our achievements and get closer to our long term goals.

We must balance our time and money to achieve our goals. This can adversely affect our family life and our health if we are not careful. There is only so much you can do. Everyone needs time away from the every day life to spend time with his or her family and friends. It is healthy! It is necessary! It gives you an opportunity to clear your mind, relax, enjoy, reduce stress, and reflect on the things you have and enjoy.

Family needs and financial needs dictate our priorities most of the time. It's a balancing act. You must give up time with your family to make money or give up making more money to be with your family. Choose your "time" wisely; a shorter period of quality time is far better than a longer period of time.

You may have to give up some time in the short term to have quality time in the future. But, keep in mind that the future will change and may not last as long as you think. You may lose the opportunity you thought you would have. Relationships change, priorities change, and situations change, the future plans cannot be so far in the future you can't see them. Sometimes the little things mean more than the big plans.

It's a trade off. We trade time with our families to earn more money, so we can spend time with our families on vacation. Always set a little money aside, just a little each check, it will grow over time. People plan differently for vacations, some don't plan at all. Vacations should be a priority everyone needs a break. It doesn't have to be an expensive trip just time with the family away from every day activities. Remember: "pay yourself first"

"Unexpected / Expected"

Most things are expected. The only thing unexpected is when they will occur. If you own an automobile, house, or anything mechanical you can "expect" it to breakdown sometime. The only thing "unexpected" is when it will breakdown. Plans must be made prior to the expected breakdown to deal with the breakdown before it happens. If you are not prepared to make adjustments for the breakdown, life will become more complicated and out of balance.

Things happen to us all of the time, some good some bad. We always tend to call the bad things "unexpected" because we failed to plan for them. Life happens for a reason, it's our fate, our direction in life. Some things we can control other things we have no control of.

Look around, how many unexpected things happen to other people that you had expected to happen. When someone wins a prize they say, "I did not expect to win". They do not say, "this was unexpected, I don't know what I'm going to do". Bad things are unexpected because we did not plan for them.

If we do not practice our religious faith, we can expect to have no direction in life. If we do not take care of our health, we can expect to have health problems. If we do not take care of our relationships, we cannot expect to have any. If we do not take care of our financial obligations, we can expect to be financially obligated. We must balance all of these things to enjoy life and be happy. Remember: "nothing is unexpected".

PART III

Balancing

"Balancing"

The more balanced your life is the happier you will be. There are many aspects in your life to balance. When we set priorities we are balancing our lives. When we have problems or setbacks we discuss our problems with others. We decide how to make adjustments to correct these setbacks, that's balancing our life.

You must try to balance everything in your life. The more things in your life that are balanced the less stress you will have and the happier you will be. The better your relationships will be.

When you lose your direction in life or you just don't feel like something is going right. Take some time to yourself and review the aspects of your life. Think about your actions or lack of actions, what you did or should have done. Ask yourself if your priorities match your goals.

Is your faith in God still strong or do you need to review his teachings, read the bible, pray for direction, or express your appreciation for the people in your life and the things you have.

Are you taking care of your health? Have things gotten so stressful that you can't sleep, eat, or you don't feel like doing anything? Exercise is a good way to relieve stress and reflect on your life while setting goals for improvement of your physical condition. This will strengthen your body and mind.

Share your thoughts with your friends and family. They care about you and love you or they wouldn't be your friends. They can give you a third person point of view, offer a second opinion, or support your decision.

Are you setting money aside for expected financial issues? If your budget is out of balance it needs to be corrected immediately. Money issues will not get better by themselves, they will only get worse.

You have to have a clear direction for your life, good health, support from your family and friends, and a balanced budget to balance your life. When your life is balanced you will feel a sense of accomplishment, comfort, security, and happiness. When we have happiness we share it with others. Remember true happiness is only achieved when we share it with someone. Remember: "you are responsible for your actions or lack of action"

"Doing Right"

Another situation that adds stress to your life is honesty, truthfulness, and doing the right thing. Doing the right thing is not always easy to do but it is always right to do the right thing. You can't go wrong doing right.

Sometimes in the short term doing the right thing may not seem to be the best thing to do. But if you don't do the right thing all of the time it will come back to haunt you in the long term. You will not know when or where but understand it is coming.

Remember you can't lie to yourself. You may be able to lie to some people and others may not believe you all of the time but others know when you are lying. One of the people, who always knows when you are lying, every time you lie, is yourself. Even when you lie to yourself you try to justify why by making excuses or blaming someone or something else. It is often easier to make excuses than to make adjustments or take responsibility for your actions.

It is not easy to be a "do righter" all of the time. You have to get in the habit of doing right all of the time. After time you do right without any hesitation and never give any thought to doing anything else. When you do right it may not be the most popular action at the time, due to the emotions and people involved. But as time passes and emotions calm down things look a little different. The right thing is still the right thing. People may not agree or like what the right thing is. But if you are fair and consistent to everyone they don't have to like your decision, but they know they were treated fairly. Remember "you can't go wrong, doing right"

"Happiness"

Life should bring you happiness. You should enjoy living life. If you are unhappy, your life is out of balance, and you need to get it in balance.

I have seen people at their best and at their worst. I have seen low income people who are happy with a positive attitude. I have seen high-income people who are very unhappy and were mad at the world. I have seen people who have lost everything. They were happy for the things they still had, their life and family. While others have had very minor damage or loss and they would rant and rave and complain about everything.

We receive happiness when we share it with others. When we do something for someone else or help someone. Knowing we helped them or that we made them happy makes us happy. Happiness we keep to ourselves may be satisfying but it doesn't truly make us happy until we share it with others.

Happiness comes in many different forms; when we help our friends or a friend admires our accomplishments. When a child admires their parents or a parent admires their child's accomplishments.

Some people are happiest when they have something to do or somewhere to be, with very little down time. Other people prefer more down time, without all of the hustle and bustle. But what is interesting, is the people with very little down time get more accomplished. I guess they don't have time to procrastinate. Staying busy all of the time adds stress to your life. Sometimes the added stress is worth the greater sense of accomplishment in the end.

Everyone has times in their lives when they are unhappy. Long-term happiness is more important than short-term disappointments. Disappointments are part of life but don't dwell on them. Be thankful for your long-term accomplishments. Remember: "happiness comes when it is shared with others"

"Motivation and Discipline"

Motivation and discipline work together. You must have goals and have the self-discipline to achieve your goals. As you achieve your goals, set new ones. As this process repeats itself, it gives you motivation.

You can get support from your family and friends to help with keeping you motivated. But the bottom line is you are responsible for your own motivation through self-discipline.

People who want to quit smoking or want to loose weight often say it's too hard. I'm not saying it is easy to quit smoking or loose weight. What I am saying is you'll never be able to achieve these goals without the self-discipline to follow the program.

When you make your mind up to achieve your goals and stick to the plan you will succeed. If you only follow the plan when someone is watching you, the plan will not fail; you failed to follow the plan.

You know when you are doing your best. If you get in the habit of disciplining yourself to always doing your best, you will never fail. Only you know what your best is. Remember you cannot lie to yourself. It takes time to develop self-discipline but once you get in that habit. It's hard to understand why other people cannot discipline themselves.

Remember: "its got to happen in your mind, before it can happen with the body"

PART IV

Major Events in my Life

"Major Events In My Life"

August 1977

I joined a volunteer Fire Department on the recommendation of a close friend. Prior to this I did not have any interest in the Fire Service. My close friend explained the things that Fire Departments do, besides putting out fires. I am a hands on type person and he thought that I would enjoy the different activities associated with the Fire Service. We are still close friends and have been like brothers for over 30 years.

This was a turning point in my life. I was 20 years old, in college studying to be an architect. I never considered the Fire Service as a career. After I got involved in the Fire Service my interest began to grow. I enjoyed the challenge of fighting fire. There were so many different things to learn. I found many things of interest. Tactics and strategy, hydraulics, and apparatus were my main interest then and they still are today.

November 1980

After I had worked in a pizza restaurant for several years, the owner was going to open a second restaurant. He asked me if I wanted to manage the restaurant or be a part owner of the second restaurant. After months of talking about it the second restaurant was never opened. So I decided to start my own pizza business. The only preparations I had were experience, ideas, and support from my friends and family. I searched for a location and building, priced equipment, and formulated my ideas. After I obtained an estimate of expenses I applied for a business loan. Once it was approved I began to search for deals on equipment. I found a location and worked with the landlord to modify the building to meet my plans and the requirements of the health department. I designed a logo, menus, obtained a liquor license, found food distributors, hired employees, and established "Firehouse Pizza"

This was a goal I set in my life before I entered the Fire Service. I had left the job at the pizza restaurant and left college to work full time in a factory. I did this to earn more money so I could set more money aside to start Firehouse Pizza. I continued working as a volunteer Firefighter and working until I saved enough money to start my own business. It was a lot of work but I was totally responsible for the operation of the business. I had to prepare the food, order supplies, train employees, ensure that everything was kept clean, complete a work schedule for employees, and balance the books daily. This was an opportunity for me to apply my strategies and ideas for business. Also I had to learn managing and relating to employees.

March 1982

I enjoyed running my own business. Firehouse Pizza was located in a new and developing area. When the home building slowed down so did business. I closed and sold Firehouse Pizza after almost a year and a half of operation. I decided to pursue a career in the Fire Service.

This was a difficult decision to make. I was proud of my accomplishment of starting my own business. I enjoyed making pizzas, relating to the public, operating the business, and managing employees. I felt that I would be a failure by closing the business I had worked so hard to establish. I could have stayed and invested more money. I decided to pursue the Fire Service.

January 1983

After applying and testing for several Fire Departments I was accepted to the Fire Academy of a Fire Department out of state. I was working in a gas station while I applied to several Fire Departments. Some were not accepting applications, others accepted applications but were not hiring. I tested for three Fire Departments. I made two eligibility lists. One Fire Department out of state accepted me into their Fire Academy. This would mean I would have to move away from my friends and family to an area I knew nothing about. I decided to accept the position and start a new life and career.

January 1983

A week after being accepted to the Fire Academy I was involved in a fire truck accident. There were three of us on the apparatus. I broke my back, one Firefighter had minor injuries, and the other Firefighter died 9 ½ hours later from his injuries. The Firefighter that died and myself were close friends and had just finished working out at the gym when we received the emergency call. It was unknown if I would be able to accept the position on the Fire Department or even walk again. It was also unknown if I would ever be able to return to the Fire Service. I had 11 ½ hours of surgery the first time to repair my fractured and dislocated back.

This was probably the most traumatic time of my life. I was excited about finally getting a full time Fire Department job, when everything changed. I broke my back, lost a close friend, could not walk, and was unable to report to the Fire Academy. I remember lying in the emergency room and hearing my mother crying in the waiting room. I asked the nurse to let her in so I could talk to her. I told my mother "I was fine I just broke my back". Later I was transferred to another hospital because my injuries were so severe and the other hospital could provide better treatment. At that hospital I was in the emergency room with my father. They were busy. So I had to wait, that upset my father. I told my father "my injuries are not life threatening". At that time I was not aware of how serious my injuries were. The prognosis was not good. It was believed that I would be paralyzed from the waist down. I laid in the hospital for a week before surgery while they were running tests, reviewing x-rays, and deciding what to do. I was asked several times what I wanted to do if I could not be a firefighter. I said: "I want to be a firefighter". I was in the hospital a total of 25 days. After surgery I wanted to try to walk. They would not let me try until the Doctor said I could. It hurt to sit in a chair because I had been lying flat for so long. Once I could sit in a chair for an hour I was able to attempt walking. I was not allowed to walk without someone with me at all times so I would not fall. I walked 4 times a day in the spinal cord unit with crutches. I had to wear a back brace for 6 months after surgery and used crutches to walk. After the stay in the hospital I was transferred to rehab. I spent 35 days in rehab lifting weights, walking, and doing various therapies for my legs and back. I was determined to be a firefighter or at least the best I could be. After a lot of rehab and work I returned to firefighting after 8 months with two steel rods in my back.

January 1984

After a year I returned to the hospital for a second surgery to remove the steel rods from my back. The second surgery took 4 ½ hours. The bone had healed so well they had to chip bone away from the rods to remove them.

By this time I was back fighting fires locally without any problems. It took time to gain confidence in my back again. I was afraid of injuring it again and not being able to heal as well. But as time went on I began to worry less about injuring my back. I kept in contact with the Fire Academy out of state. I sent my records to them and told them I am still interested in the position on the Fire Department. I was finally given a date to report to the academy.

June 1984

I had provided medical updates to the Fire Department and I was accepted for the job again. After passing another physical exam I moved to another state to accept a paid position on a paid Fire Department.

After I completed the 12 weeks of training in the Fire Academy and passed all of the tests I became a Firefighter. Once I was assigned to a Station I returned to my old home to move all of my belongings to my new home. I had finally achieved my goal of being a paid Firefighter. October 1986 After I completed my training in the Fire Academy I began to build a new life. I bought an older house that required some work. I enjoy doing home improvements and this gave me an opportunity to own a house and make improvements. During this time I got married and we decided to start a family.

December 1990

I graduated from college with a degree in Fire Science. I started college in 1975 and attended two years but did not achieve a degree. I decided to return to college 1987 to complete a degree in Fire Science. I took two classes at a time until I completed my degree while working two jobs.

January 1991

Started a family after many attempts. My first son was born premature and required special care for over six months. He stayed in the hospital for three months before we could bring him home. He eventually out grew the seizures and sleep apnea.

During his stay in the hospital, we visited him twice a day. He could not breathe on his own, so he was on a respirator. We talked to him, to let him know that we were there. The Doctors said he had to come off the respirator. It was unknown if he was strong enough to breathe on his own. This was a difficult time because it took us so long to get to this point. Due to complications, we miscarried during previous pregnancies. Now we finally have a son and he is having difficulties. We felt helpless. We spent as much time with him as we could. One night after we had talked to him, he took himself off the respirator. He continued to improve and grow stronger and we finally brought him home.

May 1992

My wife became pregnant again, and added a second son to our family. This time we did not have all of the complications we had the first time. He was healthy!

1992 – 1994

After completing college I continued taking classes and earning certifications. I also studied for promotional tests. I was promoted to Fire Lieutenant and certified as an Emergency Medical Technician, Hazardous Materials Technician, and Instructor. I was also certified nationally for Officer II, Instructor III, and Driver. All of this training helped to advance my career and income.

August 1999

My wife moved out and filed for divorce. We were married almost 13 years, had two boys, and owned a new house. When they left so did my family. My family is important to me. I had been working to provide for my family and to invest in our future.

I went from a family of four to living alone. I also felt that my boys were taken away from me. My wife decided to leave; the boys had to go because of my work schedule. We spent time together doing several activities. We built different things, attended scouts, and they were on a baseball team. I continued to spend as much time as I could with them. It was very difficult to adjust to this new arrangement.

July 2000

I met my future wife. She had two daughters, a little older than my boys. As our relationship grew so did the relationship between the six of us. I had to create an environment where the girls would accept me, the boys would accept my future wife, and the 4 children would accept each other.

August 2003

I got married a second time. This was a difficult decision for both of us. My wife had been married for about 11 years the first time and I had been married about 13 years the first time. Both of us had been hurt and didn't want to be hurt again. Once we developed our trust for each other, our commitment to each other grew. But our relationship included more than just the two of us. We were six! We wanted everyone to be happy. I asked my wife to marry me in front of the four children and asked for their approval before we got married. I enlarged my family and have more people to share my life.

August 2004, February 2005

My mother in-law and father in-law passed away within six months of each other. This was a tremendous loss to my wife, stepdaughters, and myself. This left a big void in our lives.

August 2005

My youngest brother passed away. I had talked with him about a week before he died and all was well. We were talking about things in our lives and getting together. We lived 750 miles apart. It was difficult to coordinate work and school schedules to visit each other. I often recall things we did together while we were younger and what he would think of current events.

Summary

As we go through life things happen. How we react to these situations directly affect our lives. We can make life more complicated or keep it simple. The better our lives are balanced the better we can handle events in our lives. Things happen for a reason. When one door closes another door opens. You cannot give up. You are the only one who can balance your life.

I have always tried to make wise decisions. I look at my choices, affects, and outcomes. I make the best decision I can. Some times my decisions have not been easy or the most popular. I felt they were the best decision in the long term. There are many times when my actions or lack of actions upset someone. That happens to everyone. I live my life based on my priorities, values, goals, and interests.

I have always tried to do the right thing. I set goals to keep motivated and use self-discipline to keep on track. Sharing my goals and achievements with family and friends help with balancing my life. I have always tried to keep a positive attitude and positive perspective of life. I set priorities and expect setbacks. Setbacks are just another part of life. We can only control the setbacks by living and learning from life.

I have always had religion in my life. I believe we are on earth to serve a purpose. Our purpose has a starting point and an ending point. The things that happen to us as we live our lives are predetermined by God and are our fate. Each of us are just a small part of God's master plan. We pray to God for guidance and to give him thanks. We do not know what our fate in life will be but things happen for a reason.

I have always been in good health. I continue to take care of my health. As my life has changed so has my health management. Adjustments have to be made for age, physical condition, and habits. I continue to workout with weights. I have adjusted my diet to accommodate my aging body. I try to balance work, sleep, and play to maintain good mental and physical health.

Family and friends have always been an important part of my life to share good and bad times. I have always felt the support from my family and friends. They do not always agree with me but we have always learned from each other and shared life's experiences.

From the time I was young I tried to set money aside for something in the future. When I want to purchase something I set money aside before I make the purchase. As my purchases got bigger I had to learn to make my money work for me. Regardless how much money you have you can always find something to spend it on. Because of my occupation I planned for my family first. I wanted them to be taken care of if something happened to me. My priorities in finance have not changed much over the years.

I have come up with simple quotes to keep these thoughts in my mind. Each quote is one simple thought that makes you think about a broader meaning. It also helps you plan your actions.

"Conclusion"

Follow the word of God. Pray for guidance and direction. He will show you the way. Listen to your body. Be in control of your mind and body. It will give you signs when you're out of balance. Don't ignore your body. Share your life with your friends and family. They are there to support you and share in your happiness. Be there for them to support them and share in their happiness. Always plan for the future. Plan your long-term and short-term budget. Live within your means. Don't plan or depend on money you do not have. Remember: "it is what's in your heart and mind that makes you rich, not your possessions"

Life is short. You should be happy and enjoy life everyday. If you don't enjoy life, your life is not balanced. "Life is simple", if you keep it balanced.

"Quotes to Remember"

Introduction: "life is simple, we make it complicated"

Religion: "doing right is not always easy, but it is always right"

Health: "short-term actions or lack of action, have long-term effects"

Relationships: "you learn the most, after you know it all"

Family: "the stronger the commitment, the stronger the relationship, and vice versa"

Friends: "you are given authority, you earn respect"

Finance: "we work to live, we don't live to work"

Life: "learn from the past, live for the future"

Attitude: "be a good example, you never know who is watching"

Perspective: "you cannot lie to yourself"

Priorities: "pay yourself first"

Unexpected/Expected: "nothing is unexpected"

Balancing: "you are responsible for your actions or lack of action"

Doing Right: "you can't go wrong doing right"

Happiness: "happiness comes when it is shared with others"

Motivation: "it's got to happen in your mind, before it happens with your body"

Conclusion: "it is what's in your heart and mind that makes you rich, not your possessions"

"LIFE IS SIMPLE"